The
Wishing Ship

by Nat Gabriel ∗ illustrated by Erica Magnus

MODERN CURRICULUM PRESS
Pearson Learning Group

David sat up in his bed and listened. He could hear birds singing outside his window. He could hear Ellen singing along to the radio in the kitchen. He knew she would be wearing her red bathrobe and her hair would still be wet from her morning shower. She was probably making his lunch and setting out the breakfast cereal on the counter.

David lay back on his pillow and waited for the other familiar morning sounds: Ed's shoes on the stairs as he headed down for breakfast and the screen door squeaking open and slamming shut as he let Buck, the family dog, out into the backyard. It had been the same way every morning for the past six months. David found it reassuring.

Before Ellen and Ed had become his foster parents, David had lived with other foster families. In fact, his last home had been a gigantic old farmhouse where seven other foster children had lived too. His foster parents, the Brocks, had been nice. And they'd meant well. But David often felt they didn't really have time to pay attention to him. He'd lived there for almost a year before the agency moved him to Ellen and Ed's home.

Soon Ellen would come upstairs and knock on his door. She did that every morning at exactly seven-thirty. David heard Ed let Buck into the house. He waited for the sound of Ellen's slippers scuffing up the stairs. He looked at the clock and watched the second hand make the final trip around the face.

"David? Are you up?" Ellen called from the hall.

"I'm up, Ellen!" David called back as he climbed out of bed and ran his fingers through his hair.

He looked at himself in the bathroom mirror as he washed his face and combed his hair. He wondered if they knew that today was special.

Downstairs, Ellen had put out a bowl and a spoon and a pitcher of milk for David. A cup of hot chocolate steamed in his favorite blue cup. Three boxes of cereal stood side-by-side on the counter.

"What will it be, big guy?" Ellen asked.

David chose cornflakes and poured them into the bowl. Ed sat down at the table across from David.

"Did you sleep well last night?" asked Ed.

"I slept just fine," said David.

"Really? That's surprising. I never sleep well the night before my birthday," Ellen said as she joined them at the table with her cup of coffee.

David smiled. They knew it was his birthday! Last year, at the Brocks' house, his birthday had barely been noticed.

"How would you like to celebrate your birthday, David?" asked Ellen.

"With a big cake, a mountain of presents, and enough ice cream to feed an army, I'll bet," laughed Ed.

"Actually, my mother, father, and I had a tradition on birthdays," David said.

"Really? What was it?" asked Ellen.

"Well, the person whose birthday it was would make a wish and put it in the wishing ship," said David.

"The wishing ship?" asked Ed.

"You're going to think it's silly," said David. Suddenly he wished he hadn't said anything. Cake and ice cream would have been a fine way to celebrate his birthday. Why had he brought up the wishing ship? All it did was make him miss his parents. He was filled with despair. He didn't want to spend today, his tenth birthday, thinking about his parents and the accident that had taken them away from him.

"David, you don't have to tell us if you don't want to. We can celebrate your birthday any way you want," said Ellen gently. "But if you'd like to share your family tradition with us, we'd like to hear about it."

David looked at Ellen. He looked at her long curly brown hair and her soft round pink face. He had liked her face the moment he'd set eyes on her. He'd liked Ed too. He'd liked his deep voice and the way his laugh erupted like a volcano when he was amused.

"My mother would make a boat out of newspaper," David began slowly. "She folded it in some special way and it came out looking just like a ship. Then the birthday person would draw a picture and write a birthday wish on it. Then that person would fold it up and put it inside the newspaper boat."

David paused and took a sip of his hot chocolate. Ellen and Ed waited for him to go on.

"We would get in the car and drive down to the river with the newspaper boat. We'd go to a place where the water moved quickly and there weren't any rocks or weeds. We'd set the boat in the water. Then we'd sing a song as we watched it float away," David said. He could hear the refrain in his head, hear his mother's sweet, high voice singing it. He remembered every word.

"Can you sing us the song?" asked Ellen.

"I don't remember it," said David. He just couldn't sing that song now. It would make him too sad.

Ed drove David to school. They didn't talk about the wishing ship at all.

"Ellen and I will pick you up after school today. Okay, buddy?" Ed said in his deep voice.

"Sure," said David as he grabbed his backpack and closed the car door.

"Have a good one," Ed called.

"Yeah, you too," David called back as he watched the car pull away. All during the school day the refrain of the song played in David's head. Finally the bell rang, and David pulled on his jacket and headed out to find Ed and Ellen. The old blue station wagon was first in the line of cars. Ellen waved out the window and Ed gave a quick honk of the horn. David tossed his backpack into the car and hopped in the back seat next to it.

"How was your day?" Ellen asked as she turned around in her seat and smiled at David.

Ed usually turned right at the bottom of the hill, but this time he made a left and headed in the direction of the highway.

"Where are we going?" asked David.

"We're going to the river," said Ellen.

"What river?" asked David.

"Actually, it's more of a stream, but around here it's as close as we get to a river," answered Ed.

They drove in silence for about ten minutes. Finally, Ed exited the highway and followed signs for Gallup Park.

There they parked and walked through the woods to a small stream. There was a picnic table under a gigantic pine tree. Ellen set the bag she'd been carrying on the table.

"Okay, you have to promise not to laugh," she said as she reached into the bag.

"I promise," said David.

She pulled out a folded-up piece of newspaper. The ends were covered with tape and the middle sagged a little, but you could still tell that it was supposed to be a boat.

"Not exactly perfect, is it?" said Ellen with a little sigh.

"It's great!" said David.

"It symbolizes our love, Ellen. I just hope it floats!" said Ed with a laugh.

"It does. I tested it in the bathtub," she said.

Ellen pulled out a stack of paper and some crayons and markers and set them on the table in front of David.

"Why don't you work with these for a little bit. Ed and I will check out the current and look for the perfect launching spot," Ellen said.

It was just like Ellen to realize that David needed to be alone right then. She and Ed walked hand-in-hand down the bank of the stream, while David chose a sheet of blue paper and set to work. When he finished, he carefully folded the paper and slipped it inside the lopsided boat.

"I think we found the perfect spot," called Ed.

"Bring the boat, David," Ellen called.

David picked up the boat and carried it down to the edge of the stream where Ed and Ellen were patiently waiting for him. David carefully set it in the water. Then they all watched as the current caught it and began pulling it downstream.

Ellen put her arm around David's shoulder and gave him a reassuring little squeeze. In his head the refrain of the song rose up, and without thinking about it, David began to sing softly. As the boat drifted down the stream, David's voice got stronger. By the time the boat rounded the bend and floated out of sight, he was singing the song loud and clear. It felt incredible.

Ellen had packed some sandwiches and a thermos of lemonade. She put it all out on the picnic table.

"There's a cake at home, but I was afraid it would get squished, so we'll have it when we get back," she said.

Ed gave David a small package wrapped in red paper.

"This is a tradition in my family," he said as David pulled off the paper. "My grandfather gave it to my father on his tenth birthday, who gave it to me on my tenth birthday, and now I'm giving it to you on your tenth birthday."

David looked at the old, slightly dented spyglass that Ed had given him. He felt the heat rise up in his chest.

"You should save this to give to your son. I mean, just in case you have one someday," said David.

Ed and Ellen exchanged a look.

"We'd like you to be our son," said Ed. "We'd like to ask the court if we can adopt you—if that's what you want too."

That night David lay in his bed with the spyglass tucked under his pillow. He thought about the newspaper boat and the blue sheet of paper tucked inside it. On the paper he had drawn a picture of Ellen and Ed. Next to it he'd drawn a picture of himself. *Please let me keep them*, he had written. It looked as if he was going to get his birthday wish.

As he drifted off to sleep, the refrain of the song played in his head. He could still hear his mother's sweet, high voice, but now he heard Ed and Ellen singing too. They didn't know all of the words yet. But he knew in time they would learn them.